precious knit blankies for baby

LEISURE ARTS, INC.
Little Rock, Arkansas

EDITORIAL STAFF
Editor-in-Chief: Susan White Sullivan
Knit and Crochet Publications Director:
   Lindsay White Glenn
Director of Designer Relations: Cheryl Johnson
Special Projects Director: Susan Frantz Wiles
Senior Prepress Director: Mark Hawkins
Art Publications Director: Rhonda Shelby
Technical Editor: Linda A. Daley
Technical Writers: Sarah J. Green, Cathy Hardy,
   and Lois J. Long
Editorial Writer: Susan McManus Johnson
Art Category Manager: Lora Puls
Graphic Artists: Jacob Casleton, Kara Darling
   and Becca Snider
Imaging Technician: Stephanie Johnson
Prepress Technician: Janie Marie Wright
Photography Manager: Katherine Laughlin
Contributing Photographer: Ken West
Contributing Photo Stylist: Sondra Daniel
Publishing Systems Administrator: Becky Riddle
Mac Information Technology Specialist:
   Robert Young

BUSINESS STAFF
President and Chief Executive Officer:
   Rick Barton
Vice President of Sales: Mike Behar
Director of Finance and Administration:
   Laticia Mull Dittrich
National Sales Director: Martha Adams
Creative Services: Chaska Lucas
Information Technology Director: Hermine Linz
Controller: Francis Caple
Vice President, Operations: Jim Dittrich
Retail Customer Service Manager: Stan Raynor
Print Production Manager: Fred F. Pruss

TABLE OF CONTENTS

tri-color garter ridge throw ....page 4

zigzag carriage throw ....page 8

chunky cable blanket ....page 12

pom-pom carriage throw ....page 16

color block blanket ....page 18

gingham check blanket ....page 26

fuzzy blanket with tassels................page 30

reversible blanket with bobbles........page 32

lace car seat blankie ....page 36

ribbed blankie.................................page 40

mitered squares throw ....page 42

slip stitch blankie.............................page 46

basket weave blankie.......................page 50

striped patchwork blanket...............page 54

cabled comfort carriage throw.........page 58

sheep blankie.................................page 62

general instructions.........................page 67

knitting basics ....page 73

yarn information..............................page 79

Library of Congress Control Number: 2011930438

ISBN-13: 978-1-60900-126-1

So original, so adorable—blankets this warm and beautiful will be perfect for that special baby! Delight a new mom with a blanket of sweet sheep for her little lamb. Thrill a wee one with a deeply soft carriage throw that's delightful for tiny fingers to touch and pat. Jean Adel's patterns to knit are designed to make the best use of yarns that are wonderfully fluffy, superbly plush—perhaps even woven with pom-poms! These 16 small afghans are quick and easy to knit, and make truly precious gifts.

Meet Designer Jean Adel

With a background as the former Senior Editor for *Vogue Knitting International* and *Family Circle Easy Knitting* magazines, Managing Editor for Lion Brand Yarn Company, international knitwear designer, and author of *Knitted Critters for Kids to Wear*, it comes as no surprise that the next step for Jean Adel would be owning a Web business. JeanAdel.com features a line of whimsical knits for children as well as one-of-a-kind, unique and sophisticated gifts for babies, children, and home.

In keeping with Jean's love of designing, her second book, *Precious Knit Blankies for Baby* features a collection of 16 designs sure to warm the hearts of stitchers. When asked how she developed her designs for this book, Jean says, "I draw on the natural beauty of rural Pennsylvania for inspiration. I keep my designs fun, simple, and portable. Even with our hectic lives today, there are plenty of windows of opportunity to slip in rows here and there, completing these blankets in no time. Baby blankets are special because they are kept as treasured heirlooms."

Jean's love of knitting began early. "My Grandmother taught me to knit when I was five years old," she says. "I still have the needles, yarn, and that first project—a baby blanket for my doll that we made together, a memory maker I have always cherished." To learn more about Jean and her designs, visit JeanAdel.com.

tri-color garter ridge throw

Stripes of tri-colored Garter Stitch make ridges on a Stockinette Stitch background. A knit-in Garter Stitch border frames it all nicely. For a no-fuss finish, weave in the ends as you go.

■◐□□ EASY

Finished Size: 29" (73.5 cm) square

materials

Medium Weight Yarn
(3.5 ounces, 155 yards
(100 grams, 142 meters) per skein):
  White - 6 skeins
  Blue - One skein
  Gold - One skein
  Red - One skein
29" (73.5 cm) Circular knitting needle,
  size 9 (5.5 mm) **or** size needed
  for gauge
Yarn needle

GAUGE: In Body pattern,
       16 sts = 4" (10 cm) and
       24 rows = 3½" (9 cm)

Techniques Used:
Changing Colors **(Fig. 1b, page 69)**

Instructions continued on page 6.

bottom border

With White, cast on 116 sts.

Rows 1-7: Knit across.

body

Row 1 (Right side): Knit across to last 4 sts, drop White; with second White, K4.

Row 2: K4, drop White; with second White, purl across to last 4 sts, K4.

Rows 3-6: Repeat Rows 1 and 2 twice.

Row 7: K4, drop White; with Red, knit across to last 4 sts, drop Red; with second White, K4.

Row 8: K4, drop White; with Red, knit across to last 4 sts, cut Red; with second White, K4.

Row 9: K4, drop White; with Gold, knit across to last 4 sts, drop Gold; with second White, K4.

Row 10: K4, drop White; with Gold, knit across to last 4 sts, cut Gold; with second White, K4.

Row 11: K4, drop White; with Blue, knit across to last 4 sts, drop Blue; with second White, K4.

Row 12: K4, drop White; with Blue, knit across to last 4 sts, cut Blue; with second White, K4.

Repeat Rows 1-12 for pattern until piece measures approximately 28" (71 cm) from cast on edge, ending by working Row 5.

Last Row: K4, cut White; with second White, purl across to last 4 sts, K4.

top border
Rows 1-6: Knit across.

Bind off all sts in **knit**.

Make 2 pom-poms with Gold and 2 pom-poms with Red *(Figs. 9a-c, page 72)*.

Using photo as a guide for placement, attach one pom-pom to each corner of Throw.

zigzag carriage throw

This simple pattern is worked in a worsted wool yarn that shows off the stitches. The four shades keep the blanket interesting, while the self-finishing edges make this an ideal quick-knit project.

◧■□□ EASY +

Finished Size: 24½" x 28" (62 cm x 71 cm)

materials

Medium Weight Yarn ⓜ④
(4 ounces, 190 yards
(113 grams, 173 meters) per skein):
    Lt Blue - One skein
    Blue - One skein
    Lt Green - One skein
    Green - One skein
29" (73.5 cm) Circular knitting needle,
    size 8 (5 mm) **or** size needed for gauge

GAUGE: In pattern, 14 sts
        (from point to point) = 3" (7.5 cm)
        and 24 rows = 3½" (9 cm)

Techniques Used:
YO *(Fig. 2, page 69)*
K3 tog *(Fig. 5, page 70)*

Instructions continued on page 10.

throw

With Lt Blue, cast on 115 sts.

Row 1 (Right side): With Lt Blue, K2, YO, K5, K3 tog, K5, ★ YO, K1, YO, K5, K3 tog, K5; repeat from ★ across to last 2 sts, YO, K2.

Row 2: K1, purl across to last st, K1.

Rows 3 and 4: Knit across.

Rows 5-8: Repeat Rows 1-4; at end of Row 8, cut Lt Blue.

Row 9: With Blue, K2, YO, K5, K3 tog, K5, ★ YO, K1, YO, K5, K3 tog, K5; repeat from ★ across to last 2 sts, YO, K2.

Row 10: K1, purl across to last st, K1.

Rows 11 and 12: Knit across.

Rows 13-16: Repeat Rows 9-12; at end of Row 16, cut Blue.

Row 17: With Lt Green, K2, YO, K5, K3 tog, K5, ★ YO, K1, YO, K5, K3 tog, K5; repeat from ★ across to last 2 sts, YO, K2.

Row 18: K1, purl across to last st, K1.

Rows 19 and 20: Knit across.

Rows 21-24: Repeat Rows 17-20; at end of Row 24, cut Lt Green.

Row 25: With Green, K2, YO, K5, K3 tog, K5, ★ YO, K1, YO, K5, K3 tog, K5; repeat from ★ across to last 2 sts, YO, K2.

Row 26: K1, purl across to last st, K1.

Rows 27 and 28: Knit across.

Rows 29-32: Repeat Rows 25-28; at end of Row 32, cut Green.

Rows 33-192: Repeat Rows 1-32, 5 times; at end of Row 192, do **not** cut Green.

Bind off all sts in **knit**.

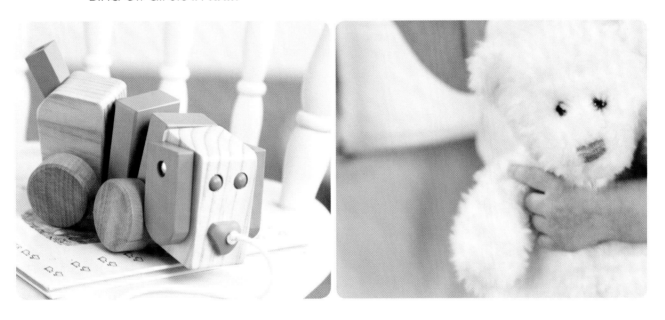

chunky cable blanket

We go fly-fishing every year on the Neshannock River, and these rolling cables remind me of the river currents—a fun, flowing texture! Chunky yarn makes for a quick knit project and an easy introduction to cables. The contrasting, simple border frames the center cable panel, making it an easy all-in-one blanket.

 EASY

Finished Size: 24½" x 30" (62 cm x 76 cm)

materials

Bulky Weight Yarn **BULKY 5**
(4 ounces, 125 yards
(113 grams, 114 meters) per skein):
  Lime - 4 skeins
  Turquoise - 2 skeins
29" (73.5 cm) Circular knitting needle,
  size 10½ (6.5 mm) **or** size needed
  for gauge
Cable needle
Bobbins (optional)

GAUGE: In Body pattern,
        18 sts and 20 rows = 4" (10 cm)

Techniques Used:
Changing Colors (*Fig. 1b, page 69*)

stitch guide . . . .
CABLE (uses 8 sts)
Slip next 4 sts onto cable needle and hold in **back** of work, K4 from left needle, K4 from cable needle.

Instructions continued on page 14.

bottom border

With Turquoise, cast on 110 sts.

Rows 1-9: Knit across.

body

Row 1 (Right side): K7, drop Turquoise; with Lime, knit across to last 7 sts, drop Lime; with second Turquoise, K7.

Row 2: K7, drop Turquoise; with Lime, purl across to last 7 sts, drop Lime; with second Turquoise, K7.

Rows 3-8: Repeat Rows 1 and 2, 3 times.

Change colors in same manner throughout.

Row 9: K7; with Lime, K 10, work Cable, (K9, work Cable) 4 times, K 10; with second Turquoise, K7.

Row 10: K7; with Lime, purl across to last 7 sts; with second Turquoise, K7.

Row 11: K7; with Lime, knit across to last 7 sts; with second Turquoise, K7.

Row 12: K7; with Lime, purl across to last 7 sts; with second Turquoise, K7.

Rows 13-16: Repeat Rows 11 and 12 twice.

Repeat Rows 9-16 for pattern until piece measures approximately 28½" (72.5 cm) from cast on edge, ending by working Row 15.

Last Row: K7, cut Turquoise; with Lime, purl across to last 7 sts, cut Lime; with second Turquoise, K7.

top border
Rows 1-8: Knit across.

Bind off all sts in **knit**.

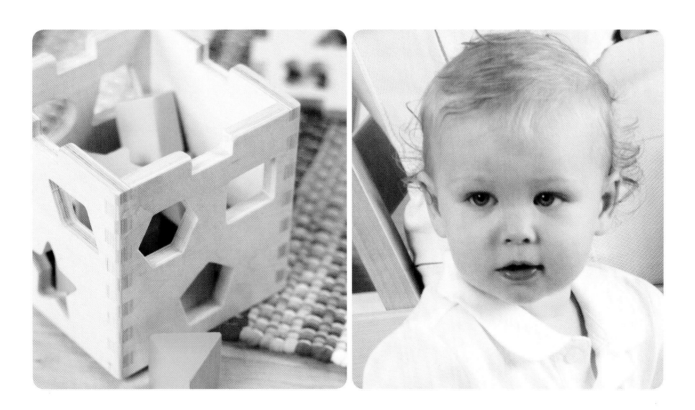

pom-pom
carriage
throw

In late spring, the countryside abounds with delicious strawberries. The "berry" texture in this throw is created when you use pom-pom yarn worked in Garter Stitch. It's warm and easy to care for, and it knits up in no time!

■□□□ **BEGINNER**

Finished Size: 24" x 25" (61 cm x 63.5 cm)

materials

SUPER BULKY **6**

Super Bulky Weight Novelty Yarn
(3.5 ounces, 54 yards
(100 grams, 50 meters) per skein):
  6 skeins
29" (73.5 cm) Circular knitting needle,
  size 9 (5.5 mm) **or** size needed
  for gauge

GAUGE: In Garter Stitch (knit every row),
         12 sts and 12 rows = 4" (10 cm)

Work the yarn in between the "pom-poms" and do **not** pull the "pom-poms" through the stitch on the needle.

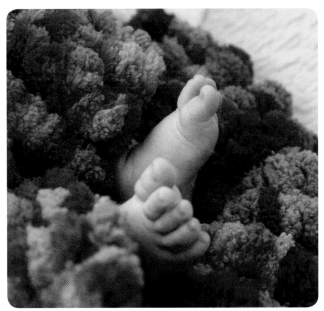

throw

Cast on 72 sts.

Knit every row (Garter Stitch) until Throw measures approximately 25" (63.5 cm) from cast on edge.

Bind off all sts in **knit**.

. . . .

color block blanket

Comfortable cotton yarn is trans-seasonal, taking Baby from cool summer evenings into fall. The blanket is worked in two-tone blocks of Seed Stitch and Stockinette Stitch, making five separate vertical strips that are joined together. When changing colors, be sure to twist yarns on the wrong side to prevent holes in your work.

◼◼◻◻ **EASY +**

Finished Size: 35" x 44½" (89 cm x 113 cm)

materials

Medium Weight Yarn **MEDIUM 4**
(3.5 ounces, 207 yards
(100 grams, 188 meters) per skein):
 Gold - 2 skeins
 Burnt Orange - 2 skeins
 Green - 2 skeins
 Off-White - 2 skeins
Straight knitting needles, size 8 (5 mm)
 or size needed for gauge
Bobbins (optional)
Yarn needle

GAUGE: In Seed Stitch,
 17 sts and 29 rows = 4" (10 cm)
 One Strip = 7" (17.75 cm) wide

Techniques Used:
Changing Colors *(Fig. 1b, page 69)*

Instructions continued on page 20.

strip #1

block one

With Burnt Orange, cast on 30 sts.

Row 1 (Right side): (K1, P1) across.

Row 2: (P1, K1) across.

Rows 3-8: Repeat Rows 1 and 2, 3 times.

Row 9: K1, (P1, K1) twice, drop Burnt Orange; with Gold, knit across to last 5 sts, drop Gold; with second Burnt Orange, P1, (K1, P1) twice.

Row 10: P1, (K1, P1) twice, drop Burnt Orange; with Gold, purl across to last 5 sts, drop Gold; with second Burnt Orange, K1, (P1, K1) twice.

Rows 11-38: Repeat Rows 9 and 10, 14 times; at end of Row 38, cut Gold.

Row 39: K1, (P1, K1) twice, knit across to last 5 sts, cut Burnt Orange; with second Burnt Orange, P1, (K1, P1) twice.

Rows 40-46: Repeat Rows 2-8; at end of Row 46, cut Burnt Orange.

block two

Row 1 (Right side): With Gold, knit across.

Row 2: (P1, K1) across.

Row 3: (K1, P1) across.

Rows 4-8: Repeat Rows 2 and 3 twice, then repeat Row 2 once **more**.

Change colors in same manner throughout.

Row 9: K1, (P1, K1) twice; with Green, knit across to last 5 sts; with second Gold, P1, (K1, P1) twice.

Row 10: P1, (K1, P1) twice; with Green, purl across to last 5 sts; with second Gold, K1, (P1, K1) twice.

Rows 11-38: Repeat Rows 9 and 10, 14 times; at end of Row 38, cut Green.

Row 39: K1, (P1, K1) twice, knit across to last 5 sts, cut Gold; with second Gold, P1, (K1, P1) twice.

Rows 40-46: Repeat Rows 2-8; at end of Row 46, cut Gold.

blocks three thru seven

Using Placement Diagram as a guide for color placement, repeat Rows 1-46 of Block Two for the remaining 5 Blocks.

Bind off all sts in pattern.

placement diagram

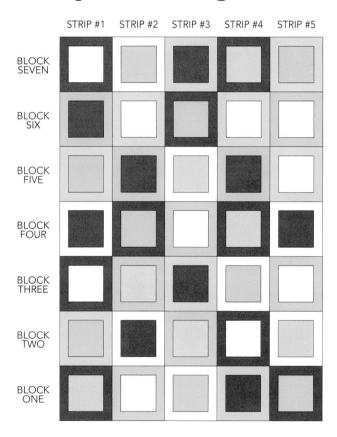

Instructions continued on page 22.

strip #2

block one

With Green, cast on 30 sts.

Row 1 (Right side): (K1, P1) across.

Row 2: (P1, K1) across.

Rows 3-8: Repeat Rows 1 and 2, 3 times.

Row 9: K1, (P1, K1) twice; with Off-White, knit across to last 5 sts; with second Green, P1, (K1, P1) twice.

Row 10: P1, (K1, P1) twice; with Off-White, purl across to last 5 sts; with second Green, K1, (P1, K1) twice.

Rows 11-38: Repeat Rows 9 and 10, 14 times; at end of Row 38, cut Off-White.

Row 39: K1, (P1, K1) twice, knit across to last 5 sts, cut Green; with second Green, P1, (K1, P1) twice.

Rows 40-46: Repeat Rows 2-8; at end of Row 46, cut Green.

block two

Row 1 (Right side): With Off-White, knit across.

Row 2: (P1, K1) across.

Row 3: (K1, P1) across.

Rows 4-8: Repeat Rows 2 and 3 twice, then repeat Row 2 once **more**.

Row 9: K1, (P1, K1) twice; with Burnt Orange, knit across to last 5 sts; with second Off-White, P1, (K1, P1) twice.

Row 10: P1, (K1, P1) twice; with Burnt Orange, purl across to last 5 sts; with second Off-White, K1, (P1, K1) twice.

Rows 11-38: Repeat Rows 9 and 10, 14 times; at end of Row 38, cut Burnt Orange.

Row 39: K1, (P1, K1) twice, knit across to last 5 sts, cut Off-White; with second Off-White, P1, (K1, P1) twice.

Rows 40-46: Repeat Rows 2-8; at end of Row 46, cut Off-White.

blocks three thru seven

Using Placement Diagram as a guide for color placement, repeat Rows 1-46 of Block Two for the remaining 5 Blocks.

Bind off all sts in pattern.

strip #3

block one

With Off-White, cast on 30 sts.

Row 1 (Right side): (K1, P1) across.

Row 2: (P1, K1) across.

Rows 3-8: Repeat Rows 1 and 2, 3 times.

Row 9: K1, (P1, K1) twice; with Green, knit across to last 5 sts; with second Off-White, P1, (K1, P1) twice.

Row 10: P1, (K1, P1) twice; with Green, purl across to last 5 sts; with second Off-White, K1, (P1, K1) twice.

Rows 11-38: Repeat Rows 9 and 10, 14 times; at end of Row 38, cut Green.

Row 39: K1, (P1, K1) twice, knit across to last 5 sts, cut Off-White; with second Off-White, P1, (K1, P1) twice.

Rows 40-46: Repeat Rows 2-8; at end of Row 46, cut Off-White.

block two

Row 1 (Right side): With Green, knit across.

Row 2: (P1, K1) across.

Row 3: (K1, P1) across.

Rows 4-8: Repeat Rows 2 and 3 twice, then repeat Row 2 once **more**.

Row 9: K1, (P1, K1) twice; with Gold, knit across to last 5 sts; with second Green, P1, (K1, P1) twice.

Row 10: P1, (K1, P1) twice; with Gold, purl across to last 5 sts; with second Green, K1, (P1, K1) twice.

Rows 11-38: Repeat Rows 9 and 10, 14 times; at end of Row 38, cut Gold.

Row 39: K1, (P1, K1) twice, knit across to last 5 sts, cut Green; with second Green, P1, (K1, P1) twice.

Rows 40-46: Repeat Rows 2-8; at end of Row 46, cut Green.

blocks three thru seven

Using Placement Diagram as a guide for color placement, repeat Rows 1-46 of Block Two for the remaining 5 Blocks.

Bind off all sts in pattern.

Instructions continued on page 24.

strip #4

block one

With Gold, cast on 30 sts.

Row 1 (Right side): (K1, P1) across.

Row 2: (P1, K1) across.

Rows 3-8: Repeat Rows 1 and 2, 3 times.

Row 9: K1, (P1, K1) twice; with Burnt Orange, knit across to last 5 sts; with second Gold, P1, (K1, P1) twice.

Row 10: P1, (K1, P1) twice; with Burnt Orange, purl across to last 5 sts; with second Gold, K1, (P1, K1) twice.

Rows 11-38: Repeat Rows 9 and 10, 14 times; at end of Row 38, cut Burnt Orange.

Row 39: K1, (P1, K1) twice, knit across to last 5 sts, cut Gold; with second Gold, P1, (K1, P1) twice.

Rows 40-46: Repeat Rows 2-8; at end of Row 46, cut Gold.

block two

Row 1 (Right side): With Burnt Orange, knit across.

Row 2: (P1, K1) across.

Row 3: (K1, P1) across.

Rows 4-8: Repeat Rows 2 and 3 twice, then repeat Row 2 once **more**.

Row 9: K1, (P1, K1) twice; with Off-White, knit across to last 5 sts; with second Burnt Orange, P1, (K1, P1) twice.

Row 10: P1, (K1, P1) twice; with Off-White, purl across to last 5 sts; with second Burnt Orange, K1, (P1, K1) twice.

Rows 11-38: Repeat Rows 9 and 10, 14 times; at end of Row 38, cut Off-White.

Row 39: K1, (P1, K1) twice, knit across to last 5 sts, cut Burnt Orange; with second Burnt Orange, P1, (K1, P1) twice.

Rows 40-46: Repeat Rows 2-8; at end of Row 46, cut Burnt Orange.

blocks three thru seven

Using Placement Diagram as a guide for color placement, repeat Rows 1-46 of Block Two for the remaining 5 Blocks.

Bind off all sts in pattern.

strip #5

block one

With Burnt Orange, cast on 30 sts.

Row 1 (Right side): (K1, P1) across.

Row 2: (P1, K1) across.

Rows 3-8: Repeat Rows 1 and 2, 3 times.

Row 9: K1, (P1, K1) twice; with Green, knit across to last 5 sts; with second Burnt Orange, P1, (K1, P1) twice.

Row 10: P1, (K1, P1) twice; with Green, purl across to last 5 sts; with second Burnt Orange, K1, (P1, K1) twice.

Rows 11-38: Repeat Rows 9 and 10, 14 times; at end of Row 38, cut Green.

Row 39: K1, (P1, K1) twice, knit across to last 5 sts, cut Burnt Orange; with second Burnt Orange, P1, (K1, P1) twice.

Rows 40-46: Repeat Rows 2-8; at end of Row 46, cut Burnt Orange.

block two

Row 1 (Right side): With Off-White, knit across.

Row 2: (P1, K1) across.

Row 3: (K1, P1) across.

Rows 4-8: Repeat Rows 2 and 3 twice, then repeat Row 2 once **more**.

Row 9: K1, (P1, K1) twice; with Gold, knit across to last 5 sts; with second Off-White, P1, (K1, P1) twice.

Row 10: P1, (K1, P1) twice; with Gold, purl across to last 5 sts; with second Off-White, K1, (P1, K1) twice.

Rows 11-38: Repeat Rows 9 and 10, 14 times; at end of Row 38, cut Gold.

Row 39: K1, (P1, K1) twice, knit across to last 5 sts, cut Off-White; with second Off-White, P1, (K1, P1) twice.

Rows 40-46: Repeat Rows 2-8; at end of Row 46, cut Off-White.

blocks three thru seven

Using Placement Diagram as a guide for color placement, repeat Rows 1-46 of Block Two for the remaining 5 Blocks.

Bind off all sts in pattern.

assembly

With corresponding color, sew Strips together using Placement Diagram as a guide, page 21.

gingham check blanket

A true classic, gingham check looks good on everything from sweaters and socks to baby blankets. This beauty works up in one piece in no time with the yarn held double-strand, alternating and combining two different colors to create the "Gingham Check" effect. Accent the edges with an easy two-tone fringe.

◼◼◻◻ **EASY +**

Finished Size: 32¾" x 35¾" (83 cm x 91 cm)

materials

Medium Weight Yarn 〔**4**〕
(3.5 ounces, 205 yards
(100 grams, 187 meters) per skein):
  Blue - 5 skeins
  White - 5 skeins
29" (73.5 cm) Circular knitting needle,
  size 11 (8 mm) **or** size needed
  for gauge
Crochet hook (for adding fringe)

Blanket is knit holding two strands of yarn together throughout.

GAUGE: In Stockinette Stitch
      (knit one row, purl one row),
      11 sts and 16 rows = 4" (10 cm)

Techniques Used:
Changing Colors *(Fig. 1b, page 69)*

Instructions continued on page 28.

blanket

With two strands of Blue yarn held together, cast on 18 sts; ★ with one strand **each** of Blue and White yarn held together, cast on 18 sts; with two strands of Blue yarn held together, cast on 18 sts; repeat from ★ once **more**: 90 sts.

Row 1 (Right side): K 18, drop Blue/Blue; ★ with Blue/White, K 18; with Blue/Blue, K 18; repeat from ★ once **more**.

Row 2: P 18, drop Blue/Blue; ★ with Blue/White, K 18; with Blue/Blue, K 18; repeat from ★ once **more**.

Rows 3-24: Repeat Rows 1 and 2, 11 times.

Row 25: With Blue/White, K 18; ★ with White/White, K 18; with Blue/White, K 18; repeat from ★ once **more**.

Row 26: P 18, drop Blue/White; ★ with White/White, P 18; with Blue/White, P 18; repeat from ★ once **more**.

Rows 27-48: Repeat Rows 25 and 26, 11 times.

Rows 49-143: Repeat Rows 1-48 once, then repeat Rows 1-47 once **more**.

Bind off all sts in pattern.

fringe

Cut a piece of cardboard 3" (7.5 cm) wide and 5" (12.5 cm) long. Holding one strand of Blue and one strand of White yarn together, wind the yarn **loosely** and **evenly** lengthwise around the cardboard until the card is filled, then cut across one end; repeat as needed.

Hold 4 strands together (2 strands of **each** color); fold in half. With **wrong** side of short edge facing and using a crochet hook, draw the folded end up through a stitch and pull the loose ends through the folded end *(Fig. A)*; draw the knot up **tightly** *(Fig. B)*. Repeat, spacing fringe approximately every 3 stitches.

Lay Blanket flat on a hard surface and trim the ends.

Fig. A

Fig. B

fuzzy blanket with tassels

Let the fluffy texture of the yarn do all the work! Holding two strands together makes this design extra-plush. Simple black tassels offer a dramatic contrast. This blanket can also double as a play mat.

Finished Size: 26" x 33" (66 cm x 84 cm)

materials

Bulky Weight Yarn **5**
(1.75 ounces, 90 yards
(50 grams, 83 meters) per ball):
    White - 10 balls
Medium Weight Yarn **4**
    Black - 85 yards (77.5 meters)
29" (73.5 cm) Circular knitting needle,
    size 13 (9 mm) **or** size needed
    for gauge
Yarn needle

Blanket is knit holding two strands of Bulky Weight Yarn together throughout.

GAUGE: In Garter Stitch (knit every row), 11 sts and 16 rows = 4" (10 cm)

blanket

With two strands of White Bulky Weight Yarn held together, cast on 71 sts.

Knit every row (Garter Stitch) until Blanket measures approximately 33" (84 cm) from cast on edge.

Bind off all sts in **knit**.

With Black Medium Weight Yarn, make 4 Tassels and attach one to each corner of Blanket *(Figs. 8a & b, page 71)*.

reversible blanket with bobbles

My garden is bursting with lilies, gladiolus, and poppies all summer long, so I like how this bright, reversible blanket keeps the feel of a summer garden year-round. The top and bottom pieces are seamed together, creating a double thickness.

◼◼◻◻ EASY

Finished Size: 26" x 30" (66 cm x 76 cm)

materials
Bulky Weight Yarn **BULKY 5**
(1.75 ounces, 90 yards
(50 grams, 83 meters) per ball):
  Pink - 6 balls
  Orange - 6 balls
29" (73.5 cm) Circular knitting needle,
  size 11 (8 mm) **or** size needed
  for gauge
Yarn needle

GAUGE: In Garter Stitch (knit every row),
        12 sts and 20 rows = 4" (10 cm)

Techniques Used:
K2 tog *(Fig. 3, page 70)*
Slip 1, K1, PSSO *(Figs. 4a & b, page 70)*

Instructions continued on page 34.

body (Make 2)
(Make one with Pink & one with Orange)

Cast on 78 sts.

Knit every row (Garter Stitch) until piece measures approximately 30" (76 cm) from cast on edge.

Bind off all sts in **knit**.

bobble (Make 240)
(Make 120 with Pink & 120 with Orange)

With color indicated and leaving a 6" (15 cm) length for sewing, cast on one st.

Row 1: (K, P, K, P, K) **all** in same st: 5 sts.

Rows 2 and 3: K5.

Row 4: K2 tog twice, K1: 3 sts.

Row 5: Slip 1 as if to **knit**, K1, PSSO, K1: 2 sts.

Row 6: K2 tog; cut yarn leaving a 6" (15 cm) length for sewing, pull end through remaining st.

finishing

Sew Orange Bobbles randomly to Pink Body.
Sew Pink Bobbles randomly to Orange Body.

With **wrong** sides together and matching sts and rows, sew Body pieces together around all 4 sides.

lace car seat blankie

Reminiscent of violets, this pretty little blankie is ideal for the brisk days of early spring. The easy Tulip Lace pattern and delicate seed stitch border are knit in one piece for no-fuss finishing.

 **EASY +**

Finished Size: 22" x 23" (56 cm x 58.5 cm)

materials

Medium Weight Yarn
(1.75 ounces, 90 yards
(50 grams, 82 meters) per ball):
  Lavender - 4 balls
  Purple - 2 balls
29" (73.5 cm) Circular knitting needle,
  size 8 (5 mm) **or** size needed
  for gauge

GAUGE: In pattern,
      16 sts and 24 rows = 4" (10 cm)

Techniques Used:
Changing Colors *(Fig. 1b, page 69)*
YO *(Fig. 2, page 69)*
K2 tog *(Fig. 3, page 70)*
Slip 1, K1, PSSO *(Figs. 4a & b, page 70)*

Instructions continued on page 38.

bottom border

With Purple, cast on 89 sts.

Rows 1-6: K1, (P1, K1) across.

body

Row 1 (Right side): K1, (P1, K1) twice, drop Purple; with Lavender, knit across to last 5 sts, drop Lavender; with second Purple, K1, (P1, K1) twice.

Change colors in same manner throughout.

Row 2 AND ALL WRONG SIDE ROWS: K1, (P1, K1) twice; with Lavender, purl across to last 5 sts; with second Purple, K1, (P1, K1) twice.

Row 3: K1, (P1, K1) twice; with Lavender, K3, YO, slip 1 as if to **knit**, K1, PSSO, ★ K6, YO, slip 1 as if to **knit**, K1, PSSO; repeat from ★ across to last 7 sts, K2; with second Purple, K1, (P1, K1) twice.

Row 5: K1, (P1, K1) twice; with Lavender, K1, K2 tog, YO, K1, YO, slip 1 as if to **knit**, K1, PSSO, ★ K3, K2 tog, YO, K1, YO, slip 1 as if to **knit**, K1, PSSO; repeat from ★ across to last 6 sts, K1; with second Purple, K1, (P1, K1) twice.

Row 7: K1, (P1, K1) twice; with Lavender, K3, YO, slip 1 as if to **knit**, K1, PSSO, ★ K6, YO, slip 1 as if to **knit**, K1, PSSO; repeat from ★ across to last 7 sts, K2; with second Purple, K1, (P1, K1) twice.

Row 9: K1, (P1, K1) twice; with Lavender, knit across to last 5 sts; with second Purple, K1, (P1, K1) twice.

Row 11: K1, (P1, K1) twice; with Lavender, K7, ★ YO, slip 1 as if to **knit**, K1, PSSO, K6; repeat from ★ across to last 5 sts; with second Purple, K1, (P1, K1) twice.

Row 13: K1, (P1, K1) twice; with Lavender, K5, K2 tog, YO, K1, YO, slip 1 as if to **knit**, K1, PSSO, ★ K3, K2 tog, YO, K1, YO, slip 1 as if to **knit**, K1, PSSO; repeat from ★ across to last 10 sts, K5; with second Purple, K1, (P1, K1) twice.

Row 15: K1, (P1, K1) twice; with Lavender, K7, ★ YO, slip 1 as if to **knit**, K1, PSSO, K6; repeat from ★ across to last 5 sts; with second Purple, K1, (P1, K1) twice.

Row 17: K1, (P1, K1) twice; with Lavender, knit across to last 5 sts; with second Purple, K1, (P1, K1) twice.

Repeat Rows 2-17 for pattern until piece measures approximately 22" (56 cm) from cast on edge, ending by working Row 9 or Row 17.

Next Row: K1, (P1, K1) twice, cut Purple; with Lavender, purl across to last 5 sts, cut Lavender; with second Purple, K1, (P1, K1) twice.

top border
Rows 1-6: K1, (P1, K1) across.

Bind off all sts in pattern.

ribbed blankie

Fresh as a spring rain over a scattering of wildflowers, the hand-painted yarn I used for this throw has a fuzzy texture, creating a misty effect. With easy 2 x 2 ribbing and having no borders, this pattern is an ideal first project.

■■□□ EASY

Finished Size: 26" x 32" (66 cm x 81.5 cm)

materials

Medium Weight Yarn **MEDIUM 4**
(1.75 ounces, 88 yards
(50 grams, 80 meters) per skein):
   10 skeins
29" (73.5 mm) Circular knitting needle,
   size 8 (5 mm) **or** size needed
   for gauge

GAUGE: In pattern,
         26 sts and 22 rows = 4" (10 cm)

blankie

Cast on 168 sts.

Row 1 (Right side): K1, P2, (K2, P2) across to last st, K1.

Row 2: P1, K2, (P2, K2) across to last st, P1.

Repeat Rows 1 and 2 for pattern until Blankie measures approximately 32" (81.5 cm) from cast on edge, ending by working Row 2.

Bind off all sts in pattern.

mitered squares throw

Inspired by Amish quilts, these mitered squares are easy to make by decreasing the center stitch. Create it as large or as small as you like, in stripes, two-tone, or solid colors. Mix and match to create a one-of-a kind sampler that's all your own.

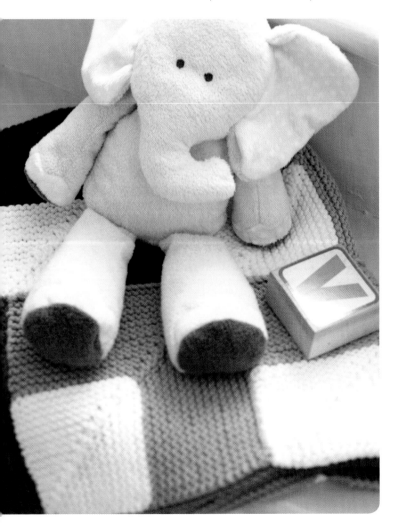

Finished Size: 25½" x 32" (65 cm x 81.5 cm)

materials
MEDIUM 4

Medium Weight Yarn
(3.5 ounces, 207 yards
(100 grams, 188 meters) per skein):
  White - One skein
  Green - One skein
  Blue - One skein
  Rose - One skein
  Gold - One skein
  Burnt Orange - One skein
  Wine - One skein
  Lt Rose - One skein
Straight knitting needles, size 8 (5 mm)
  or size needed for gauge
Marker
Yarn needle

GAUGE: In Garter Stitch (knit every row),
        16 sts and 40 rows = 4" (10 cm)
        One Square = 6³/₈" (16.25 cm)

Techniques Used:
K3 tog (*Fig. 5, page 70*)
Slip 1, K2 tog, PSSO (*Figs. 6a & b, page 70*)

Instructions continued on page 44.

square (Make 20)

For Rows 1-27, work 2 Squares using Rose and 3 Squares **each** using Green, Blue, Gold, Burnt Orange, Wine and Lt Rose.

With color indicated, cast on 61 sts.

Row 1: K 29, place marker *(see Markers, page 68)*, knit across.

Row 2 (Right side - Decrease row): Knit across to within 3 sts of marker, slip 1 as if to **knit**, K2 tog, PSSO, remove marker, K1, place marker, knit across: 59 sts.

Row 3: Knit across.

Rows 4-27: Repeat Rows 2 and 3, 12 times: 35 sts.

Rows 28-56: With White, repeat Rows 2 and 3, 14 times; then repeat Row 2 once **more**: 5 sts.

Row 57: Knit across removing marker.

Row 58: K1, slip 1 as if to **knit**, K2 tog, PSSO, K1: 3 sts.

Row 59: Knit across.

Row 60: K3 tog: one st.

Cut yarn; pull yarn end through remaining stitch and tighten to secure end.

Using Placement Diagram as a guide, sew Squares together with corresponding color.

placement diagram

slip stitch blankie

This one is excellent for summer evenings because of its cool cotton yarn! The simple Slip Stitch pattern combines with the variegated yarn to create texture and color galore! The knit-in border makes for a simple all-in-one project.

Finished Size: 24" x 32" (61 cm x 81.5 cm)

materials

MEDIUM **4**

Medium Weight Yarn
(3.5 ounces, 140 yards
(100 grams, 128 meters) per hank):
  Cream - 5 hanks
  Variegated - 4 hanks
29" (73.5 cm) Circular knitting needle,
  size 7 (4.5 cm) **or** size needed
  for gauge
Bobbin (optional)

GAUGE: In Body pattern,
          19 sts and 29 rows = 4" (10 cm)

Techniques Used:
Changing Colors *(Fig. 1b, page 69)*

Instructions continued on page 48.

bottom border

With Cream, cast on 110 sts.

Row 1 (Right side): (K1, P1) across.

Row 2: (P1, K1) across.

Rows 3-12: Repeat Rows 1 and 2, 5 times.

body

When instructed to slip a stitch, always slip as if to **purl**.

Row 1: (K1, P1) 4 times, drop Cream; with Variegated, knit across to last 8 sts, drop Variegated; with second Cream, (K1, P1) 4 times.

Row 2: (P1, K1) 4 times, drop Cream; with Variegated, purl across to last 8 sts, drop Variegated; with second Cream, (P1, K1) 4 times.

Row 3: K1, (P1, K1) 4 times, slip 1 with yarn in back, (K1, slip 1 with yarn in back) across to last 10 sts, K2, drop Cream; with second Cream, (K1, P1) 4 times.

Row 4: (P1, K1) 4 times, drop Cream; with second Cream, (K1, slip 1 with yarn in front) across to last 10 sts, K2, (P1, K1) 4 times.

Repeat Rows 1-4 for pattern until piece measures approximately 30" (76 cm) from cast on edge, ending by working Row 1.

Next Row: (P1, K1) 4 times, cut Cream; with Variegated, purl across to last 8 sts, cut Variegated; with second Cream, (P1, K1) 4 times.

top border

Row 1: (K1, P1) across.

Row 2: (P1, K1) across.

Rows 3-12: Repeat Rows 1 and 2, 5 times.

Bind off all sts in pattern.

basket
weave
blankie

I love the look of antique baskets and enjoy collecting them, so I think this large "basket-weave" pattern makes a sweet country-style blankie. And because it uses a soft and lofty merino wool, held double strand, it knits up in no time. The basket-weave panel is framed with a knit-in garter stitch border.

■□□ **EASY**

Finished Size:
 28½" x 32½" (72.5 cm x 82.5 cm)

materials

MEDIUM 4

 Medium Weight Yarn
 (3.5 ounces, 210 yards
 (100 grams, 192 meters) per skein**):**
  5 skeins
 29" (73.5 cm) Circular knitting needle,
  size 10 (6 mm) **or** size needed
  for gauge

Blankie is knit holding two strands of yarn together throughout.

GAUGE: In Body pattern,
   12 sts and 18 rows = 4" (10 cm)

Instructions continued on page 52.

bottom border

With two strands of yarn held together, cast on 86 sts.

Rows 1-12: Knit across.

body

Row 1 (Right side): Knit across.

Row 2: K6, purl across to last 6 sts, K6.

Row 3: K8, P4, (K2, P4) across to last 8 sts, K8.

Row 4: K6, (P2, K4) across to last 8 sts, P2, K6.

Row 5: K8, P4, (K2, P4) across to last 8 sts, K8.

Row 6: K6, (P2, K4) across to last 8 sts, P2, K6.

Row 7: Knit across.

Row 8: K6, purl across to last 6 sts, K6.

Row 9: K6, P3, K2, (P4, K2) across to last 9 sts, P3, K6.

Row 10: K9, P2, (K4, P2) across to last 9 sts, K9.

Row 11: K6, P3, K2, (P4, K2) across to last 9 sts, P3, K6.

Row 12: K9, P2, (K4, P2) across to last 9 sts, K9.

Repeat Rows 1-12 for pattern until piece measures approximately 30½" (77.5 cm) from cast on edge, ending by working Row 2 or Row 8.

top border
Rows 1-12: Knit across.

Bind off all sts in **knit**.

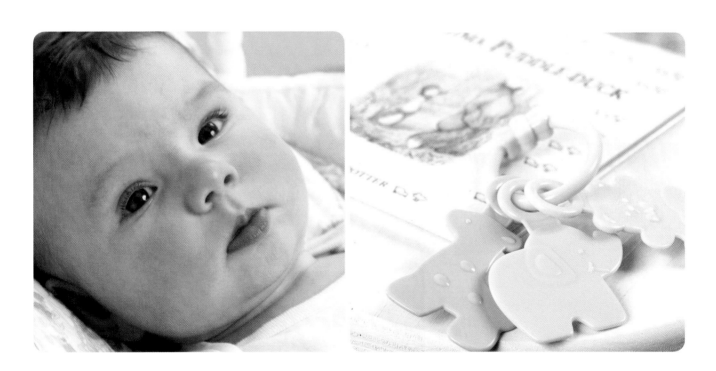

striped patchwork blanket

Antique quilts inspired this patchwork blanket. It's made of small Stockinette Stitch squares sewn together in alternating directions. A Garter Stitch border frames it all nicely. The pattern is ideal for on-the-run stitching. Add squares if you want to make your blanket bigger.

◼◼◻◻ **EASY**

Finished Size: 27" x 33" (68.5 cm x 84 cm)

materials

MEDIUM **4**

Medium Weight Yarn
(4 ounces, 190 yards
(113 grams, 173 meters) per skein):
  Pink - One skein
  Blue - One skein
  Yellow - One skein
  Green - One skein
  Off-White - One skein
Straight knitting needles, size 8 (5 mm)
  or size needed for gauge
Yarn needle

GAUGE: In Stockinette Stitch
(knit one row, purl one row),
18 sts and 24 rows = 4" (10 cm)
Each Square = 6" (15.25 cm)

Techniques Used:
Picking Up Sts *(Figs. 7a & b, page 71)*

Instructions continued on page 56.

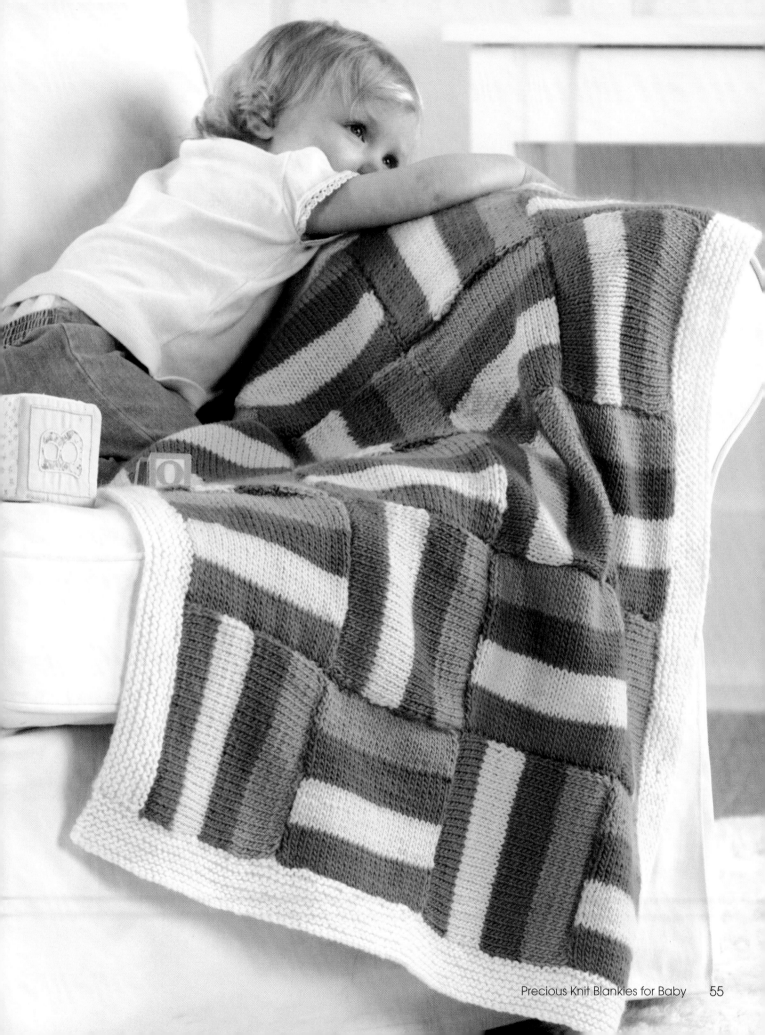

square (Make 20)

With Pink, cast on 27 sts.

Row 1: Purl across.

Row 2 (Right side): Knit across.

Rows 3-9: Repeat Rows 1 and 2, 3 times; then repeat Row 1 once **more**.

Row 10: With Blue, knit across.

Rows 11-18: Repeat Rows 1 and 2, 4 times.

Row 19: With Yellow, purl across.

Row 20: Knit across.

Rows 21-27: Repeat Rows 1 and 2, 3 times; then repeat Row 1 once **more**.

Row 28: With Green, knit across.

Rows 29-35: Repeat Rows 1 and 2, 3 times; then repeat Row 1 once **more**.

Bind off all sts in **knit**.

Using Placement Diagram as a guide, sew Squares together with corresponding color.

placement diagram

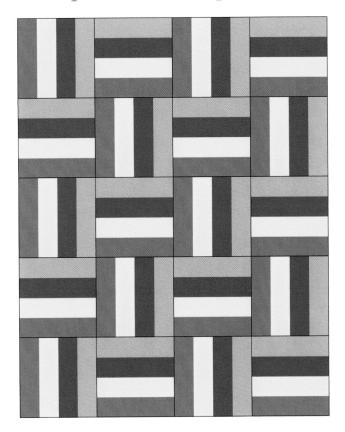

finishing
side border
With **right** side of long edge facing and using Off-White, pick up 26 sts evenly spaced across each Square: 130 sts.

Rows 1-12: Knit across.

Bind off all sts in **knit**.

Repeat across opposite long edge.

end border
With **right** side of short edge facing and using Off-White, pick up 6 sts across end of rows on Side Border, pick up 26 sts evenly spaced across each Square to opposite Side Border, pick up 6 sts across end of rows on opposite Side Border: 116 sts.

Rows 1-12: Knit across.

Bind off all sts in **knit**.

Repeat across opposite short edge.

cabled
comfort
carriage
throw

Winter white is elegant and just right for holiday gift-giving and wrapping baby in style! The simple pattern is a great introduction to cabling. Worked in super soft merino, it holds stitch definition beautifully. This throw is knit in one piece with ribbed top and bottom borders and has matching tassels on its corners.

◖■☐☐ **EASY +**

Finished Size: 26¾" x 31½" (68 cm x 80 cm)

materials

Medium Weight Yarn **④** MEDIUM
(1.4 ounces, 87 yards
(40 grams, 80 meters) per skein):
   12 skeins
29" (73.5 cm) Circular knitting needle,
   size 8 (5 mm) **or** size needed for
   gauge
Cable needle
Yarn needle

GAUGE: In Body pattern,
           23 sts and 25 rows = 4" (10 cm)

stitch guide....................

CABLE (uses 6 sts)
Slip next 3 sts onto cable needle
and hold in **front** of work, K3 from left
needle, K3 from cable needle.

Instructions continued on page 60.

Instructions continued on page 60.

bottom border

Cast on 155 sts.

Row 1: P1, (K1, P1) across.

Row 2: K1, (P1, K1) across.

Rows 3-6: Repeat Rows 1 and 2 twice.

body

Row 1 (Right side): P1, (K6, P3, K2, P3) across.

Row 2: (K3, P2, K3, P6) across to last st, K1.

Rows 3 and 4: Repeat Rows 1 and 2.

Row 5: P1, (work Cable, P3, K2, P3) across.

Row 6: (K3, P2, K3, P6) across to last st, K1.

Rows 7 and 8: Repeat Rows 1 and 2.

Row 9: (P3, K2, P3, K6) across to last st, P1.

Row 10: K1, (P6, K3, P2, K3) across.

Rows 11 and 12: Repeat Rows 9 and 10.

Row 13: (P3, K2, P3, work Cable) across to last st, P1.

Row 14: K1, (P6, K3, P2, K3) across.

Rows 15 and 16: Repeat Rows 9 and 10.

Repeat Rows 1-16 for pattern until piece measures approximately 30½" (77.5 cm) from cast on edge, ending by working Row 8 or Row 16.

top border

Row 1: P1, (K1, P1) across.

Row 2: K1, (P1, K1) across.

Rows 3-6: Repeat Rows 1 and 2 twice.

Bind off all sts in pattern.

Make 4 Tassels and attach one to each corner of Throw *(Figs. 8a & b, page 71)*.

sheep blankie

What a dreamy way to fall asleep, surrounded by cuddly sheep! This design is perfect for a boy or a girl—you only need to change the color to suit your taste. It is knitted in one piece, with the Garter Stitch border framing the Stockinette Stitch panel. The fluffy intarsia sheep have Satin Stitch faces and feet.

■■□□ **EASY +**

Finished Size: 25½" x 24" (65 cm x 61 cm)

materials

Medium Weight Yarn **4** MEDIUM
(4 ounces, 190 yards
(113 grams, 173 meters) per skein):
  Gold - 3 skeins
  Black - small amount
Bulky Weight Yarn **5** BULKY
(1.76 ounces, 72 yards
(50 grams, 66 meters) per skein):
  White - One skein
29" (73.5 cm) Circular knitting needle,
  size 8 (5 mm) **or** size needed
  for gauge
Yarn needle
Bobbins - 6

GAUGE: Using Medium Weight Yarn,
      in Stockinette Stitch, 18 sts and
      24 rows = 4" (10 cm)

Techniques Used:
Changing Colors **(Figs. 1a & b,
page 69)**

Instructions continued on page 64.

bottom border

With Gold, cast on 114 sts.

Rows 1 and 2: (K1, P1) across.

Rows 3 and 4: (P1, K1) across.

Rows 5-12: Repeat Rows 1-4 twice.

body

Row 1 (Right side): (K1, P1) across.

Row 2: K1, (P1, K1) 4 times, purl across to last 10 sts, (K1, P1) 5 times.

Row 3: P1, (K1, P1) 4 times, knit across to last 10 sts, (P1, K1) 5 times.

Row 4: (P1, K1) 5 times, purl across to last 9 sts, K1, (P1, K1) 4 times.

Row 5: (K1, P1) 5 times, knit across to last 9 sts, P1, (K1, P1) 4 times.

Rows 6-12: Repeat Rows 2-5 once, then repeat Rows 2-4 once **more**.

Each Sheep is knit using a separate bobbin. Wind approximately 50" (127 cm) of White yarn onto each bobbin. The Gold yarn will be carried across the **wrong** side of the piece, along the back of each Sheep.

Row 13: (K1, P1) 5 times, K6; with White, K7; ★ with Gold, K8; with White, K7; repeat from ★ 4 times **more**, with Gold, K7, P1, (K1, P1) 4 times.

Row 14: K1, (P1, K1) 4 times, P7; with White, P7; ★ with Gold, P8; with White, P7; repeat from ★ 4 times **more**, with Gold, P6, (K1, P1) 5 times.

Row 15: P1, (K1, P1) 4 times, K7; with White, K7; ★ with Gold, K8; with White, K7; repeat from ★ 4 times **more**, with Gold, K6, (P1, K1) 5 times.

Row 16: (P1, K1) 5 times, P6; with White, P7; ★ with Gold, P8; with White, P7; repeat from ★ 4 times **more**, with Gold, P7, K1, (P1, K1) 4 times.

Row 17: (K1, P1) 5 times, K7; with White, K5; ★ with Gold, K 10; with White, K5; repeat from ★ 4 times **more**, with Gold, K8, P1, (K1, P1) 4 times.

Row 18: K1, (P1, K1) 4 times, P8; with White, P5, cut White; ★ with Gold, P 10; with White, P5, cut White; repeat from ★ 4 times **more**, with Gold, P7, (K1, P1) 5 times.

Row 19: P1, (K1, P1) 4 times, knit across to last 10 sts, (P1, K1) 5 times.

Row 20: (P1, K1) 5 times, purl across to last 9 sts, K1, (P1, K1) 4 times.

Row 21: (K1, P1) 5 times, knit across to last 9 sts, P1, (K1, P1) 4 times.

Row 22: K1, (P1, K1) 4 times, purl across to last 10 sts, (K1, P1) 5 times.

Rows 23-42: Repeat Rows 19-22, 5 times.

Each Sheep is knit using a separate bobbin. Wind approximately 50" (127 cm) of White yarn onto each bobbin. The Gold yarn will be carried across the **wrong** side of the piece, along the back of each Sheep.

Row 43: P1, (K1, P1) 4 times, K7; with White, K7; ★ with Gold, K8; with White, K7; repeat from ★ 4 times **more**, with Gold, K6, (P1, K1) 5 times.

Row 44: (P1, K1) 5 times, P6; with White, P7; ★ with Gold, P8; with White, P7; repeat from ★ 4 times **more**, with Gold, P7, K1, (P1, K1) 4 times.

Row 45: (K1, P1) 5 times, K6; with White, K7; ★ with Gold, K8; with White, K7; repeat from ★ 4 times **more**, with Gold, K7, P1, (K1, P1) 4 times.

Row 46: K1, (P1, K1) 4 times, P7; with White, P7; ★ with Gold, P8; with White, P7; repeat from ★ 4 times **more**, with Gold, P6, (K1, P1) 5 times.

Instructions continued on page 66.

Row 47: P1, (K1, P1) 4 times, K8; with White, K5; ★ with Gold, K 10; with White, K5; repeat from ★ 4 times **more**, with Gold, K7, (P1, K1) 5 times.

Row 48: (P1, K1) 5 times, P7; with White, P5, cut White; ★ with Gold, P 10; with White, P5, cut White; repeat from ★ 4 times **more**, with Gold, P8, K1, (P1, K1) 4 times.

Row 49: (K1, P1) 5 times, knit across to last 9 sts, P1, (K1, P1) 4 times.

Row 50: K1, (P1, K1) 4 times, purl across to last 10 sts, (K1, P1) 5 times.

Row 51: P1, (K1, P1) 4 times, knit across to last 10 sts, (P1, K1) 5 times.

Row 52: (P1, K1) 5 times, purl across to last 9 sts, K1, (P1, K1) 4 times.

Rows 53-72: Repeat Rows 49-52, 5 times.

Rows 73-120: Repeat Rows 13-60.

top border

Rows 1 and 2: (K1, P1) across.

Rows 3 and 4: (P1, K1) across.

Rows 5-12: Repeat Rows 1-4 twice.

Bind off all sts in pattern.

finishing

Thread yarn needle with a double strand of Black yarn, and using photo as a guide for placement, add satin stitch legs *(Fig. A)*.

Thread yarn needle with a double strand of Black yarn. Using photo as a guide for placement, add satin stitch "faces" and "legs", alternating placement on each row of sheep.

satin stitch

Satin Stitch is a series of straight stitches worked side-by-side so they touch but do not overlap. Come up at odd numbers and go down at even numbers *(Fig. A)*.

Fig. A

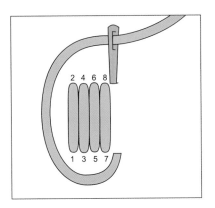

general instructions

abbreviations

cm	centimeters
K	knit
mm	millimeters
P	purl
PSSO	pass slipped stitch over
st(s)	stitch(es)
tog	together
YO	yarn over

★ — work instructions following ★ as many **more** times as indicated in addition to the first time.

( ) or **( )** — work enclosed instructions **as many** times as specified by the number immediately following **or** work all enclosed instructions in the stitch indicated **or** contains explanatory remarks.

colon (:) — the number given after a colon at the end of a row denotes the number of stitches you should have on that row.

gauge

Exact gauge is **essential** for proper size. Before beginning your project, make a sample swatch in the yarn and needles specified. After completing the swatch, measure it, counting your stitches and rows carefully. If your swatch is larger or smaller than specified, **make another, changing needle size to get the correct gauge.** Keep trying until you find the size needles that will give you the specified gauge. Once proper gauge is obtained, measure width of piece approximately every 3" (7.5 cm) to be sure gauge remains consistent.

KNIT TERMINOLOGY	
UNITED STATES	**INTERNATIONAL**
gauge =	tension
bind off =	cast off
yarn over (YO) =	yarn forward (yfwd) **or** yarn around needle (yrn)

■□□□ **BEGINNER**		Projects for first-time knitters using basic knit and purl stitches. Minimal shaping.
■■□□ **EASY**		Projects using basic stitches, repetitive stitch patterns, simple color changes, and simple shaping and finishing.
■■■□ **INTERMEDIATE**		Projects with a variety of stitches, such as basic cables and lace, simple intarsia, double-pointed needles and knitting in the round needle techniques, mid-level shaping and finishing.
■■■■ **EXPERIENCED**		Projects using advanced techniques and stitches, such as short rows, fair isle, more intricate intarsia, cables, lace patterns, and numerous color changes.

markers

As a convenience to you, we have used markers to help distinguish the beginning of a pattern. Place the markers as instructed. You may use a purchased marker or tie a length of contrasting color yarn around the needle. When you reach a marker on each row, slip it from the left needle to the right needle; remove it when no longer needed.

hints

As in all knit pieces, good finishing techniques make a big difference in the quality of the piece. Do not tie knots. Always start a new ball or skein at the beginning of a row, leaving ends long enough to weave in later. With **wrong** side facing, weave the needle through several stitches, then reverse the direction and weave it back through several stitches. When ends are secure, clip them off close to work.

KNITTING NEEDLES		
UNITED STATES	ENGLISH U.K.	METRIC (mm)
0	13	2
1	12	2.25
2	11	2.75
3	10	3.25
4	9	3.5
5	8	3.75
6	7	4
7	6	4.5
8	5	5
9	4	5.5
10	3	6
10½	2	6.5
11	1	8
13	00	9
15	000	10
17	---	12.75

Yarn Weight Symbol & Names	LACE 0	SUPER FINE 1	FINE 2	LIGHT 3	MEDIUM 4	BULKY 5	SUPER BULKY 6
Type of Yarns in Category	Fingering, size 10 crochet thread	Sock, Fingering, Baby	Sport, Baby	DK, Light Worsted	Worsted, Afghan, Aran	Chunky, Craft, Rug	Bulky, Roving
Knit Gauge Range* in Stockinette St to 4" (10 cm)	33-40** sts	27-32 sts	23-26 sts	21-24 sts	16-20 sts	12-15 sts	6-11 sts
Advised Needle Size Range	000-1	1 to 3	3 to 5	5 to 7	7 to 9	9 to 11	11 and larger

*GUIDELINES ONLY: The chart above reflects the most commonly used gauges and needle sizes for specific yarn categories.

** Lace weight yarns are usually knitted on larger needles to create lacy openwork patterns. Accordingly, a gauge range is difficult to determine. Always follow the gauge stated in your pattern.

changing colors

Wind small amounts of each color onto a bobbin to keep the different color yarns from tangling. You'll need one bobbin for each color change, except when there are so few stitches of the new color that it would be easier to carry the unused color **loosely** across the back *(Fig. 1a)*. Always keep the bobbins on the wrong side of the piece. When changing colors, always pick up the new color yarn from **beneath** the dropped yarn and keep the color which has just been worked to the left *(Fig. 1b)*. This will prevent holes in the finished piece. Take extra care to keep your tension even.

Fig. 1a

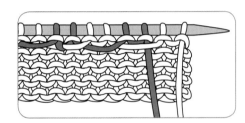

Fig. 1b

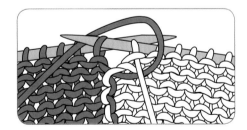

yarn over

A yarn over *(abbreviated YO)* is simply placing the yarn over the right needle creating an extra stitch. Since the yarn over produces a hole in the knit fabric, it is used for a lacy effect. On the row following a yarn over, you must be careful to keep it on the needle and treat it as a stitch by knitting or purling it as instructed.

To make a yarn over, you'll loop the yarn over the needle like you would to knit a stitch, bringing it to the front of the piece so that it will be ready to work the next stitch, creating a new stitch on the needle as follows:

Bring the yarn forward **between** the needles, then back **over** the top of the right hand needle, so that it is now in position to knit the next stitch *(Fig. 2)*.

Fig. 2

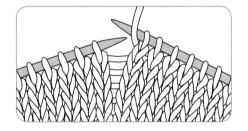

decreases
knit 2 together *(abbreviated K2 tog)*

Insert the right needle into the front of the first two stitches on the left needle as if to **knit** *(Fig. 3)*, then **knit** them together as if they were one stitch.

Fig. 3

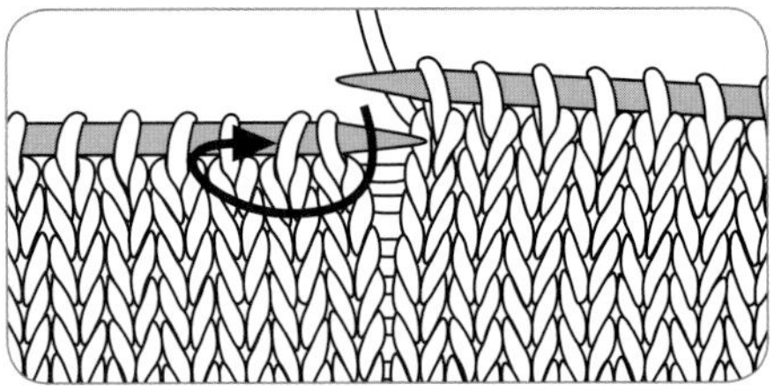

knit 3 together *(abbreviated K3 tog)*

Insert the right needle into the front of the first three stitches on the left needle as if to **knit** *(Fig. 5)*, then **knit** them together as if they were one stitch.

Fig. 5

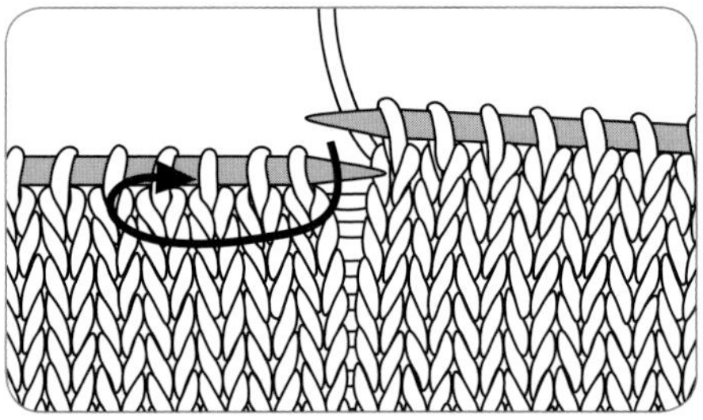

slip 1, knit 1, pass slipped stitch over
(abbreviated slip 1, K1, PSSO)

Slip one stitch as if **knit** *(Fig. 4a)*. Knit the next stitch. With the left needle, bring the slipped stitch over the knit stitch *(Fig. 4b)* and off the needle.

Fig. 4a

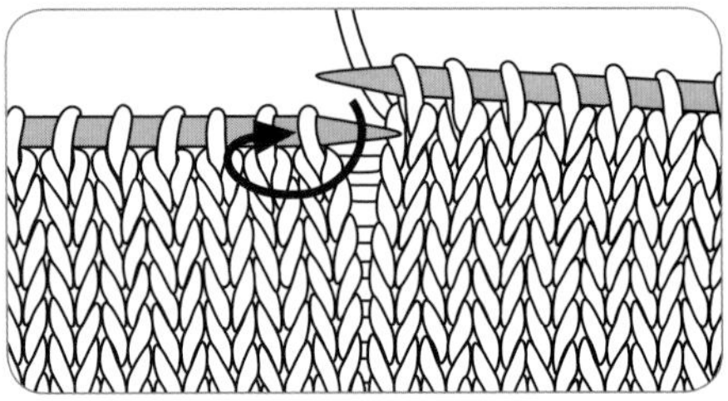

Fig. 4b

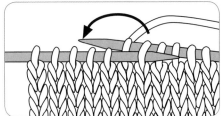

slip 1, knit 2 together, pass slipped stitch over
(abbreviated slip 1, K2 tog, PSSO)

Slip one stitch as if to **knit** *(Fig. 6a)*, then knit the next two stitches together *(Fig. 3)*. With the left needle bring the slipped stitch over the stitch just made *(Fig. 6b)* and off the needle.

Fig. 6a

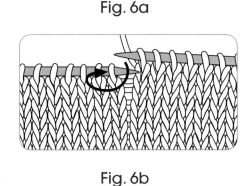

Fig. 6b

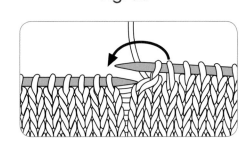

picking up stitches

When instructed to pick up stitches, insert the needle from the **front** to the **back** under two strands at the edge of the piece *(Figs. 7a & b)*. Put the yarn around the needle as if to **knit**, then bring the needle with the yarn back through the stitch to the right side, resulting in a stitch on the needle.

Repeat this along the edge, picking up the required number of stitches.

A crochet hook may be helpful to pull yarn through.

Fig. 7a

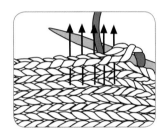

Fig. 7b

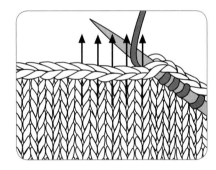

tassel

Cut a piece of cardboard 3" (7.5 cm) wide and 4" (10 cm) long. Wind a double strand of yarn lengthwise around the cardboard approximately 45 times.

Cut an 18" (45.5 cm) length of yarn and insert it under all of the strands at the top of the cardboard; pull up **tightly** and tie securely. Leave the yarn ends long enough to attach the tassel. Cut the yarn at the opposite end of the cardboard and then remove it *(Fig. 8a)*. Cut a 6" (15 cm) length of yarn and wrap it **tightly** around the tassel twice, 1" (2.5 cm) below the top *(Fig. 8b)*; tie securely. Trim the ends.

Fig. 8a

Fig. 8b

pom-pom

Cut a piece of cardboard 3" (7.5 cm) wide and as long as you want the diameter of your finished pom-pom to be.

Wind the yarn around the cardboard until it is approximately ½" (12 mm) thick in the middle *(Fig. 9a)*. Carefully slip the yarn off the cardboard and firmly tie an 18" (45.5 cm) length of yarn around the middle *(Fig. 9b)*. Leave yarn ends long enough to attach the pom-pom. Cut the loops on both ends and trim the pom-pom into a smooth ball *(Fig. 9c)*.

Fig. 9a

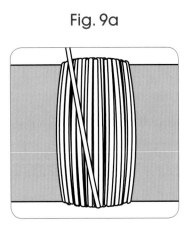

Fig. 9b

Fig. 9c

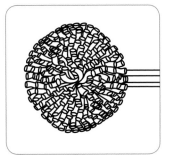

blocking

Blocking helps to smooth your work and give it a professional appearance. Check the yarn label for any special instructions about blocking.

With acrylics that can be blocked, you simply pin your Blanket to the correct size (with rust-proof pins) and cover it with dampened bath towels. When the towels are dry, the Blanket is blocked.

If the yarn is hand washable, carefully launder your Blanket using a mild soap or detergent, being careful to gently squeeze suds through the piece. Rinse it several times in cool, clear water without wringing or twisting. Remove any excess moisture by rolling it in a succession of dry terry towels. You can put it in the final spin cycle of your washer, without water. Lay the Blanket on a large towel on a flat surface out of direct sunlight. Gently smooth and pat it to the desired size. When it is completely dry, it is blocked.

Another method of blocking, that is especially good for wool, requires a steam iron or a hand-held steamer. Place the Blanket on a flat surface and pin it to the desired size. Hold the steam iron or steamer just above the Blanket and steam it thoroughly. Never let the weight of the iron touch your Blanket because it will flatten the stitches. Never steam ribbings, cables, or intricate raised patterns. Leave the Blanket pinned until it is completely dry.

knitting basics

slip knot

Step 1: Make a circle and place the working yarn (the yarn coming from the ball) under the circle *(Fig. 10a)*.

Step 2: Insert the needle under the bar just made *(Fig. 10b)* and pull on both ends of the yarn to complete the slip knot *(Fig. 10c)*. The slip knot counts as your first cast on stitch.

Fig. 10a

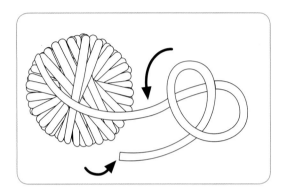

Fig. 10b

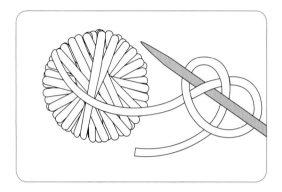

Fig. 10c

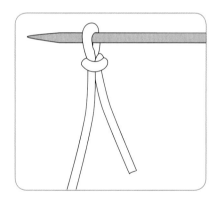

slingshot cast on

Step 1: Pull a length of yarn from the skein, allowing approximately 1" (2.5 cm) of yarn for each stitch to be cast on. Make a slip knot at the measured distance, pulling gently on both yarn ends to tighten stitch on needle.

Step 2: Hold the needle in your right hand with your index finger resting on the slip knot.

Step 3: Place the short end of the yarn over your left thumb, and bring the working yarn up and over your left index finger. Hold both yarn ends in your left palm with your 3 remaining fingers *(Fig. 11a)*.

Fig. 11a

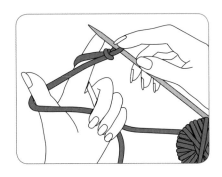

Step 4: Insert the tip of the needle **under** the first strand of yarn on your left thumb *(Fig. 11b)*.

Fig. 11b

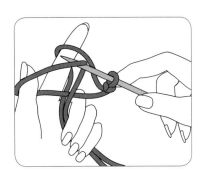

Step 5: Bring the needle **over** and around the first strand on your index finger *(Fig. 11c)*.

Fig. 11c

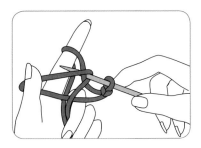

Step 6: Pull the yarn and needle down through the loop on your thumb *(Fig. 11d)*.

Fig. 11d

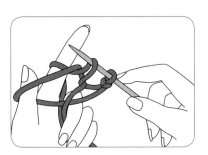

Step 7: Slip your thumb out of the loop and bring it toward you, catching the yarn end to form a new loop on your thumb *(Fig. 11e)*, and gently pulling to tighten the new stitch on the needle. Rest your index finger on the new stitch.

Fig. 11e

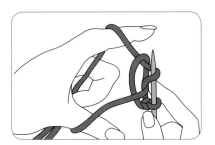

Repeat Steps 4-7 for each additional stitch.

knit stitch *(abbreviated K)*
english method

Step 1: Hold the needle with the stitches in your left hand and the empty needle in your right hand.

Step 2: With the working yarn in **back** of the needles, insert the right needle into the stitch closest to the tip of the left needle as shown in *Fig. 12a*.

Fig. 12a

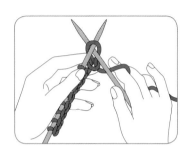

Step 3: Hold the right needle with your left thumb and index finger while you bring the yarn beneath the right needle and between the needles from **back** to **front** *(Fig. 12b)*.

Fig. 12b

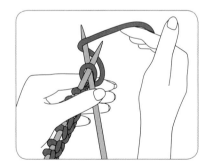

Step 4: With your right hand, bring the right needle (with the loop of yarn) toward you and through the stitch *(Figs. 12c & d)*, slip the old stitch off the left needle and gently pull to tighten the new stitch on the shaft of the right needle.

Fig. 12c

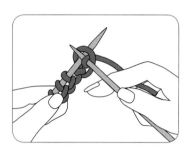

Fig. 12d

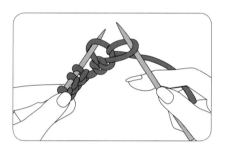

continential method

Step 1: Hold the needle with the stitches in your left hand and the empty needle in your right hand. Loop the working yarn over the index finger of your left hand and hold it loosely across the palm of your hand with your little finger.

Step 2: With the yarn in **back** of the needles, insert the right needle into the stitch closest to the tip of the left needle as shown in *Fig. 13a*.

Fig. 13a

Step 3: With your left index finger, bring the yarn between the needles from **left** to **right** around the right needle *(Fig. 13b)*.

Fig. 13b

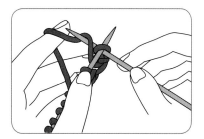

Step 4: With your right hand, bring the right needle (with the loop of yarn) toward you and through the stitch *(Figs. 13c & d)*, slip the old stitch off the left needle and gently pull to tighten the new stitch on the shaft of the right needle.

Fig. 13c

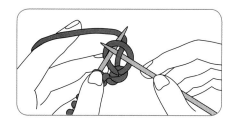

Fig. 13d

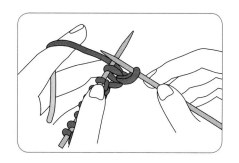

purl stitch *(abbreviated P)*
english method

Step 1: Hold the needle with the stitches in your left hand and the empty needle in your right hand.

Step 2: With the yarn in **front** of the needles, insert the right needle into the front of the stitch as shown in *Fig. 14a*.

Fig. 14a

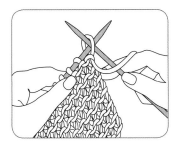

Step 3: Hold the right needle with your left thumb and index finger while you bring the yarn **between** the needles from **right** to **left** and around the right needle *(Fig. 14b)*.

Fig. 14b

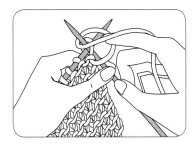

Step 4: Move the right needle (with the loop of yarn) through the stitch and away from you *(Fig. 14c)*, slip the old stitch off the left needle and gently pull to tighten the new stitch on the shaft of the right needle.

Fig. 14c

continential method

Step 1: Hold the needle with the stitches in your left hand and the empty needle in your right hand. Loop the working yarn over the index finger of your left hand and hold it loosely across the palm of your hand with your little finger.

Step 2: With the yarn in **front** of the needles, insert the right needle into the front of the stitch as show in *Fig. 15a*.

Fig. 15a

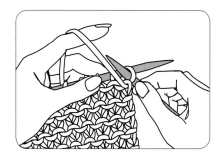

Step 3: With your left index finger, bring the yarn **between** the needles from **right** to **left** around the right needle *(Fig. 15b)*.

Fig. 15b

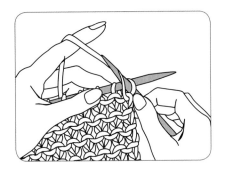

Step 4: Move your left index finger forward while moving the right needle (with the loop of yarn) through the stitch and away from you *(Fig. 15c)*, slip the old stitch off the left needle and gently pull to tighten the new stitch on the shaft of the right needle.

Fig. 15c

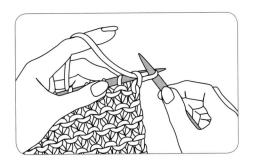

bind off

Binding off is the method used to remove and secure your stitches from the knitting needles so that they don't unravel.

Work the first two stitches.

Use your left needle as a tool to lift the second stitch on the right needle up and over the first stitch *(Fig. 16a)* and completely off the right needle *(Fig. 16b)*. Don't forget to remove the left needle from the stitch.

Fig. 16a

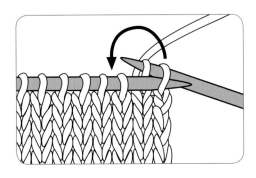

Fig. 16b

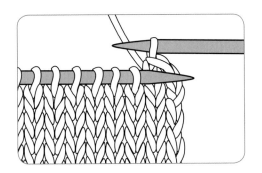

You now have one stitch on your right needle and you have bound off one stitch. Count the stitch as you bind it off, not as you work it.

Work the next stitch; you will have two stitches on your right needle. Bind off as before.

Continue until your left needle is empty and there is only one stitch left on your right needle.

Cut the yarn, leaving a long end to hide later.

Slip the stitch off the right needle, pull the end through the stitch *(Fig 16c)* and tighten the stitch.

Fig. 16c

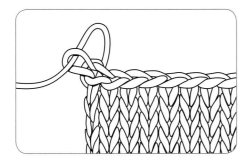

yarn information

The Blankets in this book were made using a variety of yarns. Any brand in the specified weight may be used. It is best to refer to the yardage/meters when determining how many balls or skeins to purchase. Remember, to arrive at the finished size, it is the GAUGE/TENSION that is important, not the brand of yarn.

For your convenience, listed below are the specific yarns used to create our photography models.

TRI-COLOR GARTER RIDGE THROW
Red Heart® Stitch Nation® Full O' Sheep™
White - #2205 Little Lamb
Blue - #2510 Aquamarine
Gold - #2605 Honeycomb
Red - #2910 Poppy

ZIGZAG CARRIAGE THROW
Brown Sheep Lamb's Pride Worsted
Lt Blue - #M51 Winter Blue
Blue - #M57 Brite Blue
Lt Green - #M184 Pistachio
Green - #M113 Oregano

CHUNKY CABLE BLANKET
Brown Sheep Lamb's Pride Bulky
Lime - #M120 Limeade
Turquoise - #M78 Aztec Turquoise

POM-POM CARRIAGE THROW
Red Heart® Pomp-A-Doodle™
#9955 Berries & Cream

COLOR BLOCK BLANKET
Lion Brand® Cotton-Ease®
Gold - #186 Maize
Burnt Orange - #134 Terracotta
Green - #194 Lime
Off-White - #099 Almond

GINGHAM CHECK BLANKET
Patons® Canadiana
Blue - #10725 Clearwater Blue
White - #10006 Winter White

FUZZY BLANKET WITH TASSELS
Berroco® Plush®
White - #1900 Snow White
Patons® Canadiana
Black - #10040 Black

REVERSIBLE BLANKET WITH BOBBLES
Berroco® Plush®
Pink - #1947 Bubblegum
Orange - #1920 Orange Flash

LACE CAR SEAT BLANKIE
Classic Elite® Jil Eaton CottonTail
Lavender - #7532 Plum
Purple - #7595 Violet

RIBBED BLANKIE
Brown Sheep Handpaint Originals
#HP130 Victorian Garden

MITERED SQUARES THROW
Lion Brand® Cotton-Ease®
White - #100 Snow
Green - #194 Lime
Blue - #110 Lake
Rose - #112 Berry
Gold - #186 Maize
Burnt Orange - #134 Terracotta
Wine - #195 Azalea
Lt Rose - #103 Blossom

SLIP STITCH BLANKIE
Plymouth Yarn® Fantasy Naturale
Cream - #8176 Cream
Variegated - #9610 Orange/
Yellow/Pumpkin

BASKET WEAVE BLANKIE
Patons® Classic Wool
#00210 Petal Pink

STRIPED PATCHWORK BLANKET
Brown Sheep Lamb's Pride Worsted
Pink - #M34 Victorian Pink
Blue - #M51 Winter Blue
Yellow - #M13 Sun Yellow
Green - #M16 Seafoam
Off-White - #M10 Creme

CABLED COMFORT CARRIAGE THROW
Lion Brand® Superwash Merino Cashmere
#098 Ivory

SHEEP BLANKIE
Brown Sheep Lamb's Pride Worsted
Gold - #M155 Lemon Drop
Black - #M05 Onyx
Red Heart® Buttercup™
White - #4270 White